Positive Thinking Positive Life: The Mindset
By Phil Hunter

Table of Contents

Introduction 3

What is negativity and do I suffer from it? 7

How does negativity affect behavior? 17

Acknowledge your Negative Patterns and learn how to spot them 23

    8 patterns of negative thinking.............................24

    Changing destructive thinking patterns...............27

The power of positivity 29

    How to access the power of positive thinking 36

Reprograming negative thinking patterns 39

    Step One 41

    Step Two 45

The power of self-belief and becoming the best version of yourself 49

    Why is Self-Belief important? 49

    Creating Self-Belief and Confidence 54

Find your passion in life 58

Positive thinking positive life 67

Introduction

What if I told you that happiness is a choice? What if I said you could smile and laugh more? Would you believe me? Can you remember the last time that you were truly happy or experienced the type of laughter that made your cheeks sore from smiling or brought a tear to your eye? Most likely you have experienced this type of laughter at some point in your life, but now it is a distant memory. Somewhere along the line, you lost your sense of self. You drifted slowly away from that person you were and became caught up in society's ever judging eye, telling you who you should be or how you should behave. Kind of sucks doesn't it.

Have you ever noticed children playing? They are truly joyful as they live in the moment and they are too young to have been corrupted by the social, political and cultural pressures which the world pushes on us. They enjoy the small things in life and see the world through the eyes of joy, wonder and a curiosity which keeps them entertained in a world full of unending adventures and entertainment.

The world can slowly erode you and corrupt your inner child if you let it, the negativity will creep in like damp in an old house and before you know it, you're that old man or woman at the bus stop complaining about how bad the weather is, how you regret not going travelling, how "life was so much better in my day" and you might even end up as the old man who takes the football off the kids when it lands in your garden because they are making too much of a racket and you can't hear yourself think. The good news is that it's not too late to rediscover your inner child. Like wiping dirt of a plate, you can wash away those bad habits and crippling thoughts. We cannot live our entire lives like a child playing in the mud, because that might not leave the best impression at an interview if our suit trouser legs are a mess, but when it comes to a seeing the world in a more fun and playful way, there is a lot we can learn from the children we once were. It's time to rediscover the inner child that you have forgotten and rekindle your true self by remembering that life should be a playground, it should be fun and enjoyable. I don't mean this in a spiritual, hippy, mystique kind of way, I mean it in the grounded sense that you can be happy by being yourself around others and not feel ashamed of who you are. You can be happy from just living and bettering yourself, in all areas of your life. You can learn to have fun and laugh with friends or strangers, without that feeling of self-consciousness. You can have the confidence to be yourself and enjoy whatever it is that truly ticks your boxes, floats your boat or tickles your pickle.

You need to understand and know that you are a powerful being capable of providing happiness to others by improving the journey of those around you because that is where true happiness comes from. But first you have to learn how to be happy yourself. It is in your ability to influence others by spreading your own sense of joy and happiness that will give you a sense of fulfillment. Having money and material possessions are a necessity, I don't claim that you can achieve happiness without it, because I think that is unrealistic. You need a certain amount of wealth to go after what you want in life, such as travelling, to buy a decent home for you and your family, to invest in your business ventures, to afford your children education and medical care and to treat yourself to holidays or treat your spouse to presents or gifts. The problem with money lies in placing it above everything else and chasing it like a dog chasing cars, where you are so focused on catching it, that you don't notice the scenery along the way. Seek to gain financial freedom through doing something you are passionate about, but never forget that all the wealth in the world won't give you happiness, it is in the journey, the scenery and the helping of others along the way that will bring you that. Having money is not where you are going find your spiritual fulfillment.

Jim Carey put it best when he said, "I wish people could realize all their dreams, wealth and fame, so they could see that it's not where you are going to find your sense of completion. I can tell you from experience the effect you have on others is the most valuable currency there is." He found his gift was in his ability to entertain others and bring them laughter and this is where he said he gained most joy in life. I believe everyone needs to find their own gift and use it to help others. Find your passion in life and use that passion to inspire and help others. Bring some joy to their lives and you will find you reap what you sow. I will help you find that passion and help you on your own journey to rediscover and bring back the joy to your life so, in time, you can help those around you rediscover theirs.

Unhappiness or discontent is the world's way of telling you that something is wrong. In this book, I will tell you how negativity can creep into your life and control you, if you let it. I will give you the tools to recondition your mind to spot this negativity and, in turn, replace that mentality with a positive mindset, one which will bring you the happiness and joy that has slowly diminished. It is my conviction that everyone deserves to be happy. It is not a privilege, it is a birthright. I will talk about the power of positivity and self-belief and how you can relearn to value yourself and believe in yourself to achieve your desires and dreams, all of which come from your inner thoughts and the dialogue you have with yourself on a daily basis. You don't have to go anywhere to find this happiness, it already exists within you, and all you need is to reprogram your thoughts. You can do this by buying my "Thought Modifying Inductor Ray" online for an amazing half price for a limited time only. No, I'm just kidding you, it's nothing crazy like that, reprograming is done through harnessing the use of simple psychological techniques.

First of all, let us answer some questions with all honesty, to gauge our level of happiness and see how much negativity we have let creep into our lives. Tell me, do you feel unhappy or discontent with your life? Are you stuck in a job that brings you no happiness? Do you lack the energy and motivation to change or move on? Do you keep trying to change, but sooner or later fail? If you answered yes for any of these questions, maybe it's time to try something different. Not necessarily a change in your job, house, partner or any other external factors which you may have blamed on your unhappiness, the issue lies much deeper than that. You will learn that these external factors that you think you may need are all secondary. These types of changes will be an offspring of the right mindset and will occur naturally if it truly descends from a desire to better yourself.

Sometimes we blame the external world and situations around us and get into the mindset, if only things were different or if this did not happen, then things would be so much better. What I am proposing is that we need to change this mindset and focus on what we can change, which is our perspective or our internal world. Most people know they need to change or have a desire to be better or see the world more positively, but they don't know how. What I am trying to do through this book is to help you with that process.

There's an African proverb that states, "If there is no enemy within, the enemy outside can do us no harm". What this means is that if you can control your inner thoughts and learn to handle your emotions and see things in a positive light, then the external influences, situations and negativity around you cannot control you.

I will give you the tools and equipment to help you stop letting negativity and outside influences dictate your state of mind and instead replace your inner thoughts with ones of positivity and a mindset of happiness. From this, you will learn that the universe will get out of your way and you will start to draw in positive energy and begin to notice the beauty in life, just as seeing it through the eyes of a child once more. You will learn to acknowledge negative patterns and become aware of them, so you can slowly start to replace them with happier thoughts and positive thinking and in turn you will learn the desire to better yourself and your life because you value yourself. You will be pleasantly surprised at how little internal changes will manifest themselves into positive outcomes in the external world. It all sounds very interesting doesn't it? Let's dive right in by first looking at why negativity seems so appealing.

What is negativity and do I suffer from it?

Every single day of your life you are assaulted with negativity. Negativity in work, from society, the media, cultural pressures and even your own friends and family can bombard you with negativity. Over time, if you choose to accept this negativity, it can modify the direction of your thoughts. Accepting negativity through repetition affects the subliminal and brings about a negative conviction system and you will start to become negative and contribute in its distribution. Imagine the negativity as mud, the more you play in it, the dirtier you get and the more you will spread that mud to other surfaces, objects and people you come in contact with. I think it's about time to wash those clothes and have a hot shower to get rid of that negativity once and for all? The longer you play in the mud, the more it soaks into your clothes and before long, you are wet, cold and heavy. You find it harder to move and people tend not to want to come very close to you, they may even back away from you. Same goes for negativity, the more you play in it, the more it will soak into you and define who you are, you will stand a higher chance of never getting anywhere and you will see yourself as a big muddy disappointment.

Is that who you choose to be? Is that who you have become? More importantly, is that who you *want* to be? I think for most of us, we try not to be that person, we all have that desire to improve ourselves. Let's look at how our thoughts (positive or negative) affect us.

"You are the product of your thoughts. What you think, you become".

Repeat this again to yourself three times so it sinks in. Positive or negative thoughts will define the direction your life takes. If you want something in life then think about it every day and your mind will make it a reality. Think about it carefully, the trick is *how* you think and *where* your focus lies. If you want a new car and your thoughts are, "I want a new car", "I wish I had a new car" or "I want a new car but I can't afford it", then these thoughts will remain a wish or a dream. Alternatively, if you think daily, "I am going to get a new car" or "I will save the money and get a car", then your mind will start to believe this and you will come up with ideas and ways to achieve that, such as putting money aside or getting a better job that will allow you that new car. Do you notice the subtle differences in these two ways of thinking? One says, "I want/ I wish/ I can't afford", the other says "I will get" and "I will save". These are the subtle differences in your inner thoughts that make all the difference. The former thinking is a type of negativity which you may suffer from, but not even realize.

When you nourish your brain with positive thoughts, these type of thoughts expand and grow. Encourage your brain negative thoughts and fiasco is certain to follow. So why do we incline toward the negative? Surely it makes more sense for our brain to be predisposed to positive thoughts instead of negative ones? Well positive thoughts require a certain level of consciousness and therefore more effort and energy, they require a certain inner belief system and inner dialogue that can easily be eroded by the harsh world around us.

The world is filled with daily negative bombardment. That is just the way it is unfortunately. The news on television thrives, profits and breeds from negative stories, the world is filled with hardship and struggles, people are exploited, things go wrong in life, cruelty and suffering is all around us. Society constantly chips away at our self-esteem and self-belief through its perceptions of beauty, through social, political and economic stratifications. Even the ones we surround ourselves with such as family and friends can bombard us with negative energy, knock us down and discourage us from our dreams. For these reasons, it is easy to get beat down and fall prey to losing our self-esteem because we see ourselves through the eyes of society and from those around us, eyes which are judgmental and divisive and make us feel we are not doing well enough or that we are not good enough.

For every 1 positive person, there are around 10 negative people. It is sometimes easier to "go along" with those negative people and believe what society tells us we should believe, so that we can "fit in". Conformity is a well-studied psychological phenomena. It takes a certain level of conscious awareness to notice the amount of conformity that exists (especially from our peers) and to have the strength of character to not fall privy. Overcoming conformity allows us to be who we are truly meant to be and to be proud of that person. We automatically open ourselves up to a positive view of the world, because we become comfortable in who we are, we learn to love ourselves and to go after what we want in life.

I wish Google or Microsoft would invent some positivity glasses as well as those virtual goggles they have. Just so you could see the difference in the world around you, even if it is only for a brief second, so you could glimpse what a significant impact the change in your mindset could have on the world you live in. Almost like the inverse of putting sunglasses on, instead of it being dark and monochrome, you would suddenly see brightness, colors and blinding light. Until those glasses of instant positivity and self-love are created, it will take time and effort to climb to that position of positivity, but once you are there, it is easy to stay. You will not want to take the glasses off once you put them on, for the benefits it reaps for you and your life. But you can do it, I believe in you and I think everyone has the ability to become the best version of themselves and to enjoy life.

It's always good to remember the world doesn't owe you anything. If you expected life to be easy, I'm afraid you were misinformed. That is why you must take responsibility for your life and go after what you want. Life can be a struggle and it can be hard, but there is beauty in that. Life brings many rewards through overcoming these struggles, by accomplishing your goals in the face of adversity and by sharing these accomplishments with others who are going through similar struggles because it may help them in their journey also.

So where does the seed of negativity originate? It grows in the womb of negativity of course, which is fear. Fear you are not good enough, fear of failure, fear others will judge you or not accept you and fear of pain or discomfort. Fear is the driver of negativity.

Let's use a work example of where negativity and fear affect you and why you may draw negativity into your life. Say for example, your sales numbers start dropping at work, so you lose your monthly bonuses that you have achieved in previous months. Your co-worker gets that promotion you wanted and you can tell that he/she is glad they got it instead of you. The people around you in the office, who may even be friends, they make fun of you or joke that you are slipping and you are going to get fired. They do it in jest, or just for laughs, but these negative thoughts and fears creep in and fester in your mind.

It may be easier to "fit in" by joking back and complaining about your sales figures by pointing the finger at others as the cause or by blaming the situation you are in. That is the easy way and it takes less energy to blame other people or things. After all, it's not your fault, right? So this way you don't have to do anything about it. It is easy to just go back to the group and fit in by telling them you didn't get that bonus because of so-and-so, or because the company isn't running the way it should. Or whatever other reason you might have. In many environments this is almost a socially acceptable thing to do. It is "the norm" to rant, gripe, complain and talk about how bad things are. So conforming to the social norm requires a certain amount of detachment from the situation. It moves the responsibility away from yourself and allows you to hide from your fears. Facing those fears, such as the fear you are not good enough and fear of failure is a lot harder and takes more effort and action to overcome. By avoiding your fears, you may draw negativity into your life through complaining, talking ill of others or by blaming situations. Your thoughts are focused on the negative rather the positive.

I should mention that there is nothing wrong in talking about your problems or the things that went wrong if it helps relieve the stress by working through the issue. This can be beneficial as it helps you talk through problems to come up with solutions. The problem lies in this becoming a consistent habit and in the forming of negative thinking patterns. You can talk too much about negative events to the stage where everything negative is trivial and petty and it consumes you by becoming part of your identity. When it comes to work related issues, it is always best to leave your problems at the door. A lot of problems can come from work because that is where we spend most of our time, so it is important not to carry these issues home.

What about fear and negativity in a relationship? It is wise to be aware of the ones closest to you and who you surround yourself with, for they have the greatest influence on you whether you realize it or not. "You are the average of the 5 people you spend most time with" – Jim Ron. So who do you spend most time with? Are they a positive influence on you? Are they holding you back in life because of their fears? People can often project their own fears on to you. Fear of being lonely, fear of being seen as a failure or fear of not being good enough. This can manifest itself into negativity in your life. They may do whatever they can to hold onto you, they may discourage you from following your dreams as it may lead you away from them. They may even put you down to make themselves look better or they will play on your insecurities to lower your self-esteem so that you feel you cannot get anyone better and therefore you don't leave them. They may even cause you to feel guilty or inadequate or they may be unintentionally affecting your moods by complaining a lot or bringing negativity into your life.

If you have a partner that does not encourage you in achieving your goals, or is always holding you back or bringing you down, what are your chances of having an enduring and cherishing relationship with that individual? Slim to zero would be the answer. The relationship will be based on fear and not love. The attitude you have for your partner and your behavior towards one another will have a positive or negative effect on your life. You will be with those people or at least in communication with them almost every day. Ask yourself, what value and influence are they having on your life. Are they bombarding you with negativity or positivity? What are your fears about the relationships or what do you fear most if the relationship were to end?

The principle of energy applies to both home and work relationships, it can be easier and require less energy to remember all the bad things that happened rather than remembering the positive. This is called Negative Bias and it will help you to understand why we are predisposed to the negative.

Negative Bias is an important term to be aware of and it is a known psychological term which describes the propensity for negative events or situations to have a greater effect on one's psychological state as opposed to positive or neutral ones. What this means is that if two things occur with the same intensity, one positive and one negative, a person is more likely to be impacted by the negative one. This has its roots in our evolutionary psychological development where paying more attention to negative events and situations has an evolutionary benefit for survival. Think of cavemen going out scavenging or hunting for food. They are more focused on watching out for Saber-toothed tigers lurking in the bush than going for a leisurely stroll appreciating the warm sunshine while whistling the theme tune of "The Flintstones". They were more aware of negative events such as unpleasant thoughts, emotions or social interactions and of harmful/traumatic events because this allowed them to survive longer.

Due to this inherent Negative Bias, focusing on positive events or situations like the warmth of the sun or the opening of the door by someone at the office is less likely to be remembered by the brain. You rarely here someone go home and say to their spouse, "Hey, guess what, my boss opened the door for me this morning". You are more likely to hear them say, "My boss told me I needed to have that work done by Friday, he's so bossy and he treats me unfairly". We need to prime our brain to overcome this evolutionary shortcoming so we can focus more on the positive.

Let's take a look at how negative and positive thoughts can affect you. I want you to imagine yourself as a ship sailing on water. Now imagine your brain is the bridge of that ship, where you steer and navigate. The bridge represents your conscious mind, making the decisions on what direction you take. On the ship, you have the engine room which powers the ship. The engine room is your subconscious. The sailors in the engine room do not decide on your direction, they just use the fuel to power the ship onwards. Now imagine the thoughts you have as the fuel that powers your ship in the waters of life.

Your ship can stay in safe, shallow waters and reap the rewards you already have (current possessions and situation), or you can alter the course of the ship, head a different way, where the seas are rougher but the opportunity for greater treasure is to be had. It is your choice to stay where you are or venture out and try new things and see new places. In order to do that, you need the right kind of fuel. It is positive thinking that is going to drive your ship to be more powerful and reach further out lands.

Henry Ford said, "If you always do what you've always done, you'll always get what you've always got." In order to change your thinking, you have to be willing to try something new and sail into unknown territory. What I am offering is the chance to try something different to help you. You have to give the engine room the right fuel (positive thoughts) supplied by your consciousness and this will give you the resources and power you need to push the ship onwards to unknown waters, as well as make the voyage a happier one. The fuel you provide to the engine room originates from the conscious decisions that you, as the captain, make. To have the right fuel to drive your ship and give it the power needed to reach further distances and conquer new lands and territories, you must fill your life with positive thoughts.

First you have to make the conscious decision in the bridge that you will think positive. These positive thoughts will then become habit and you start replacing the old negative wiring patterns which your brain may have become accustomed. Out with the old and in with the new. I think it's time to steer the ship into new waters and risk the unknown. It is your choice, right here, right now, to decide whether you want to follow through on a new approach to becoming a positive person or not. You have nothing to lose and everything to gain. Maybe you have already made the decision but you are not sure how to stay positive. In that case your conscious decision is to try a different approach and follow what I am proposing. You must do it with enthusiasm and passion. Make it exciting and see it as a goal you want to achieve.

I hope none of you reading this suffer from sea sickness or I have chosen a bad analogy for you, I'm sure you can still relate so just roll with it and try not to vomit over your book. If you prefer, the same principle applies to cars, just replace the ship with a car, captain with the driver, and seas with different road surfaces like tarmac and sand (shallow waters). It's your journey and your imagination, use what works for you. Take what I tell you and make it your own. I will use the ship example for this book. So back onboard your ship Captain Positivebeard, let's check where you are currently running your ship, here is a little test for you. We will find out how much negativity you actually have saturating your brain, how much it affects you and whether you are currently in shallow waters or the wide open sea. Answer the accompanying inquiries as sincerely as possible. We will expand on some of the questions I have previously asked you. On the chance that you are not totally honest with yourself while replying, then you are cheating yourself out of altering your mind set and you will keep sailing on those shallow negative waters.

- Do you find yourself thinking about how bad your life is all the time?
- Do you regularly find yourself complaining about your supervisor, boss or colleagues to your friends or spouse?
- Do you come home after a long day and complain about everything that went wrong and how you had such a rough day?
- Do you allow other people's drama into your life and let it affect you?
- Do you get caught up with the latest scandals and gossips in or outside work?
- Do you get entertainment from hearing how bad others are doing or get pleasure when you hear others are in trouble?

- Do you criticize or put others down frequently (even if you think it is just in a joking manner)?
- Do you wish you had another job or one that paid better?
- Do you have an affinity to listen to the conversations of others and make it your business to inform the world?
- Do you feel like the victim and feel that individuals are making a special effort to make your life hell?
- Do you feel that you are never in control of your own life?
- Do you cry, whine or complain to others when things are not going the way you want?
- Do you wish you had more in life or a better relationship, but feel you are stuck?

How did you get on? Did you find some of these questions resonated with you? These are only a few illustrations of the way negativity can influence you and depending on what degree the answers resonated will depend on the degree that negativity has crept into your life. It is possible your life is being controlled by negative energy and you are not as happy as you should be. Your engine room does not have the right fuel to power your ship and it is more than likely stuck on shallow waters, or even worse, stranded on the rocks.

Positive individuals, when things don't work out as expected, figure out how to get what they need to keep their ship from getting stranded. They are problem solvers. They assume responsibility and liability for their actions, and they never blame others for their situation. They understand that they alone are responsible for their life and if they want to change it, it is up to them to do something about it. Alternatively, negative people always have someone or something to blame, whether that is something that happened in their past, their upbringing, someone around them or worst of all, they blame themselves! They start to buy into the mindset that they are not good enough. They tell themselves they don't have the skills or experience, they don't have that school education that other people have, they don't have the money, they don't have the latest technology or they haven't had the best luck in life. They always find excuses. This is not the way to look at things, you are so much more than that, you deserve happiness regardless of your past or wherever you are in the present. Everyone deserves happiness. Excuses are a form of negativity, so if you accept excuses, you are accepting negativity. You need to have a "No Excuses" policy and a drive and self-belief that you *can* do it, it *is* possible, you *will* make it and you *do* deserve happiness.

It all starts with a conscious choice. If there is only one thing you take away from this book, make sure it is that you *always* have a choice. That those choices you make decide the journey you take and it is never too late to make the right choice. Define yourself by the current choices you make and not your past choices.

How does negativity affect behavior?

When it comes to behavior and attitude, the action or outcome you take will always stem from how you perceive that information internally. For example, if someone says something that you perceive as disrespectful, hateful or offensive, then you can get angry, hurt or upset and this will manifest in the associated behavioral response, such as verbally or physically lashing out, becoming withdrawn, stressed or possibly even crying like a baby and calling out for your mommy. How you perceive events internally will depend on how you perceive yourself. This is very important, so think about this carefully. If you value and respect yourself, you will always want the best for yourself. In this regard, you will take pride in what you do and you will never see yourself through the eyes of those who do not value you. You will judge yourself by your own standards, which is that you are a strong powerful being capable of inspiring others, helping them and caring for those around you. So if you see yourself as a high-value person, you will be internally calm and at peace with yourself, you will perceive things in a passive manner and not take what other people say or do personally because you do not define yourself by the standards of what others think. You will be passive in your response to these situations and you will be able to view the event objectively and you will be able to handle the situation because you have mastered your emotions.

Let's look at another example to explain more about where negativity stems from. On a social media site, someone writes a potentially harmful comment about the way you look. Why would someone do this? Why do they feel the need to put someone else down? Do you think a person who has high self-respect, self-esteem and high value for themselves would say something like this to another human being? No, of course not. Those who have love for themselves will try to encourage and inspire others. The negative comments on that social media site actually stem from the protagonist's lack of self-belief and self-respect. They try to put others down so they can feed their own ego and make themselves feel better, even if that feeling is short lived. The negative behavior stems from something that is lacking in their life and it is not, in reality, aimed at the victim, but rather themselves.

No one will ever do or say anything that is not a direct reflection of how they feel about themselves in a moment. The captain of their ship is sailing in shallow waters and will never amount to anything with the negative thoughts, attitude and fuel that powers their ship. They will never truly be happy if they do not love and respect themselves. I could go into this in a lot more detail about aggressive behavior, but I am only using this example of hostility towards others as an example of the type of information or negative assault that you might come across, there are many types of negative behaviors, such as rudeness, arrogance, bitchiness, jealousy, selfishness, intolerance and deceitfulness etc., the list goes on. It is all in how you perceive the event and more importantly how you perceive yourself that matters. Stay on the seas of positivity. Let them sail their way and you sail yours. You will see who has the better adventure and reaps the most treasures, joy and happiness. If you control your inner thoughts through your perception of yourself, then the outside world will not affect you. "If there is no enemy within, the enemy outside can do us no harm".

What is Drama and why does it appeal to us?

The definition of drama is "a story composition involving strife, action crisis, emotions and conflict, designed to be acted by players on a stage before a crowd of people". We all know somebody we'd call a Drama Queen, somebody who is a gossip or who gets involved in everyone's business or feels the need to spread that gossip to others. Drama can seem appealing to people because it makes them feel alive or important. They get to be center stage and talk or act out crazy things as it makes them feel popular or important. They need to have something going on in their life, so it's almost like they are creating intricate stories to make them feel like they have a lot going on in their own life and to get attention from others to fulfil their ego and need for self-worth. Drama helps people escape their mundane lives. This is why you need to have goals, it gives you focus and passion and you will be too concerned with trying to better your life and get happiness from this, rather than trying to "fill the void" with drama.

Drama can also stem from you not being able to handle emotions or situations. Example, your car tire blows, you're late for your meeting and your boss shouts at you. You can handle this in different ways, one of them is to act up, get frustrated or panicked and blow things up out of proportion, or the other is to realize some things are out of your control and you cannot change them and so becoming stressed and making a fuss serves no one. A strong, centered man or woman will look at the situation objectively and if it's within their power to change it, they will come up with a plan to stop it happening in the future. You should think positively how you can improve a situation and understand that things like this happen, it is to be expected. Drama is just a way of venting the frustration about not being able to cope with a situation. Believe in yourself enough to be able to handle a situation, handle your emotions and implement a plan to prevent it reoccurring, if needed. The key is to not stress about things that are out of your control and have confidence in yourself to handle matters.

How do we deal with drama?

Is it accurate to say that those always caught up in drama are not always cheerful and happy outside of that drama? Does this drama work for them in getting ahead in life and solving problems? Do they seem calm, centered and fulfilled? My experience lets me think "no." Even professional actors in television, films or plays are not excluded, some of them are not immune to leaving the drama at work and carry it on in their private life too, contributing to their negative mindsets, leading to some real life dramas.

I once heard the adage, "Enormous stuff, you're born, huge stuff, you pass on. Everything else in between is little stuff." Granted, someone's passing, getting separating/divorced, being let go from a job and enduring monetary mishaps can all be defining moments in your life that are totally reasonable to get upset about. These can be traumatic encounters that have a genuine and significant effect on our lives. The important thing to consider here is the story we append to the situation and the importance and feelings we connect with it. The common problem individuals make, when managing dramatic events, is to permit themselves to get stuck in them and to get stuck with the emotions attributed to that event to the point where it controls them. Yes, we need time to grieve, to deal with our emotions and to evaluate and take in the situation, which is a natural part of the healing process. The point where it becomes dangerous is when we let it consume our lives after this grieving period.

Some time or another, we need to deal with these emotions and handle them in a way that is positive and constructive in our lives. Bereavement is a hard situation to deal with, but a positive and grateful attitude can give us an appreciation for life. We can be glad that we knew that individual in our life and appreciate the positive influence they had on us. We can come to acceptance and realization that all beings must die. It is how you choose to live in that intervening time that matters. And if someone had a positive effect on others and enhanced their life in some way or another, then it was a life well lived.

How you feel and how you choose your attitude towards an event or situation decides your state of mind. Your state of mind then decides your activities and actions, which eventually decides the result and outcome, whether that is a positive one, a negative one or a detrimental one. There is one thing I learnt in life that changed the way I view things, which is that there is good and bad in everything, be it experience or situation. The trick is to focus on the positive and learn from the experience. It is the sign of intelligence if we can learn from the experience or mistakes of others too, that is where a wealth of experience lies. Douglas Adams put it like this, "Human beings, who are almost unique in having the ability to learn from the experience of others, are also remarkable for their apparent disinclination to do so". So a good tip for positive thinkers is to not only gain from our own experiences, but take the positive from the experience of others too.

Another place drama can originate, is from an unmet desire. You expected "A" but got "B." How you react to the sudden result will influence the effect it has on your life. How you perceive the unmet desire will create positive or negative thinking patterns. Here are several cases of unmet desires:

- You're in line for advancement and didn't get it.
- Your life partner arranged a night out with you and the sitter cancels last minute.
- You're leaving for vacation and your manager says they require you to stay.
- You expected a big prize and got a fruit basket.

You can see where I'm going here? Unexpected situations can arise and can lead to negative emotions if you let it. When you have a goal and it doesn't work out, rather than lounging around, getting furious, lashing out at somebody or feeling terrible/distraught about it, won't help. It won't change the result or take care of the issue. So as opposed to becoming involved with the drama or venting it to those around you, make an decision to move forward from it and don't dwell on those things you have no control over. Make the best of a bad situation. How we decide to react to the unmet desires will direct where you our ship sails. So whenever you are met with an unforeseen circumstance, don't turn it into drama. Stop, take a breath and remind yourself that you can learn from this and continue onwards. See it is just a small bump in the road, but it will not lead you from your path.

In life, potential drama will always be around, but you can choose how you deal with it. You can control the significance you give it and that is when potential drama can really turn out to be productive, use the unmet desire as an opportunity to see the best in all situations. Use it as a way to practice your positive mindset. The more you practice, the more it becomes a habit and the more positive fuel you will have to sail your ship wherever you desire.

Here's your assignment. I challenge you to surrender drama for the following 30 days. Quit making everything mean more than it is and blowing things out of proportion. Do not get involved in gossip, slander of others or complaining about anything and see any potential drama through passive, objective eyes and lastly, do not stress over situations you have no control over. If you have no control over it, don't get upset or angry at negative energy directed at you that arose from this type of "no control" situation. Attempt to make a dramatic story a positive experience that you can learn from. Practice the mindset of seeing the best in a bad situation. You are the captain, you can choose how you perceive information and what type of fuel you make of it.

Acknowledge your Negative Patterns and learn how to spot them

It can be extremely hard sometimes to concentrate on the good when perceived bad things are happening in your life. The good news is that you can prime your brain to concentrate on the good things throughout your life as opposed to dwelling on the bad. First, you must learn to acknowledge and spot negative patterns so that you can begin to replace them with positive ones. You cannot solve a problem if you do not know a problem exists. Even Alcoholics Anonymous at the start of their meetings, stand up and admit they are an alcoholic. They do this for a reason, it is only when you acknowledge you have a problem, that you can start your journey of recovery. Treat your negativity the same way, you are a negativoholic and you want to change. Put down that glass half empty and detox from the negative liquid in your system. You must change the way you think and change your patterns and habits that formed from the negative bombardment of the world. Let's learn how to spot the negative thinking patterns by looking out for the *8 patterns of negative thinking*.

8 patterns of negative thinking

"Life is awful" Thinking Pattern

Everything in life is terrible, everyone is not to be trusted and something bad always happen to me.

Examples: "Life sucks", "Life is just a constantly struggle", "Life always hits me the worst".

"Unconfirmed convincing" Thinking Pattern

You tend to come to conclusions with no proof or evidence of that conclusion because it is easier to think that way (negative thinking takes less effort) and you are being mentally lazy, you do not want to go through the process of problem solving the issue as that takes too much effort so you convince yourself not to do it. This can be truly damaging as it stops you seeing reality for what it is and instead keeps you locked away in your prism of negativity, where you could instead be moving ahead and facing your fears head on. You could be progressing and achieving. Examples: "I could never get that job, there will be other people better suited than me", "I'm not going to the gym today, it will be too busy", "They are probably closed at this time anyway".

"Always goes wrong" Thinking Pattern

This is where you don't think anything good will ever happen to you because it will always go wrong. This can be a detrimental state of mind where you expect failure to happen and you firmly believe you are not deserving of anything great happening to you. Examples: "There's no point getting that car, it will probably break down anyway and I'll have to spend all my money to get it fixed", "There's no point getting that car, knowing my luck, someone will scrape it or I'll crash it", "I should continue with this crappy job, I'll not be able to get a better one because knowing my luck the shop will close down", "There's no point going to the gym, I'll probably just injure myself".

"The low value/low opinion" Thinking Pattern

You assume individuals are thinking the worst about you, that they are judging you or that you are not good enough. Examples: "She probably thinks I'm fat", "She's too pretty to want to be my friend", "That girl will never like me, she's out of my league", "I'll never be able to make that football team, I'm just not good enough, those other players are far better than me".

"I should but it's just…" Thinking Pattern

This kind of individual knows what they need to do to change their life, they are very able and they know they can do it, but there's always that one thing stopping them. They would do it, if only they had… X, Y or Z. Examples: "I know I could go to college and get that degree, but I'm advancing in my job at the minute, I'll apply next year instead", "I know I could get that actor's role, but I'm still not finished my lessons yet", "I really want to go travelling, but it's just I need to finish this work experience first".

"Emotional based" Thinking Pattern

Your feelings and emotions control what you are thinking and distorts your vision of the truth. You may be a very short tempered or easily offended individual. You are quick to react to people or situations. These people especially would benefit from being calm, passive and objective, instead of quick tempered, judgmental and sensitive. They need to focus on themselves and understanding that they are powerful beings and do not judge themselves by the opinions of others. Examples: "No way would I ever do that!", "I can't believe she said that, that's it, we are done!", "This is too hard, stuff it, I'm out of here!"

"It's all my fault" Thinking Pattern

You consider yourself to be the reason for everything terrible that happens. This sort of individual does not assume liability for the good things that happen, it is only the bad things that they take responsible for. Just a point to note here, yes it is important to take responsibility for your life and the things that happen, you are steering the ship, but you can blame yourself excessively and think you are not good enough. One is taking responsibility, the other is self-loathing, so don't confuse the two. One comes from a perspective of loving yourself and wanting to improve and better yourself, the other from a perspective of fear that you are not good enough. There is a big difference here, which I hope you understand. Examples: "It's my own fault he left me for another girl, I didn't do enough to make him happy", "It's my fault he cheated, I didn't make enough effort with my looks", "It's my fault we didn't win the match, I'm too slow and heavy and I am not skillful enough".

Note: Personal responsibility could be saying "I think I am too slow, I will work on my sprinting and stamina". Self-loathing is saying "I think I am too slow because I am fat". Understand the difference between taking responsibility and always blaming yourself.

"They're all wrong" Thinking Pattern

You see everybody as unequipped for doing anything right and your way is the most ideal approach. Not to be confused with confidence and self-assuredness, which is good, alternatively these individuals can be cocky, arrogant or prideful and need humility to help them judge situations better and see things more objectively. They can be hard on others or "knock them down" or belittle them. This thinking pattern can be hardest to admit to yourself, if you suffer from it. You are probably thinking right now, "What does he know." It can be hard to spot and it is the ones closest to you that could suffer from your mindset. Be careful of your friends and partners who could be on the receiving end, don't knock their confidence or stifle their dreams because you don't believe in yourself, or you think they cannot do something because you are not able to do it. You might not say directly, "you are not good enough to get that job", but you will instead say, "You should probably stick to the job you have, the money is good". This is you projecting your own fears onto them, if you can't do it, no one can. Remember the example I gave before about haters on social media and what they say is a direct reflection of how they feel about themselves. Well this is the same idea of projection. Examples: "You shouldn't play as striker, you don't have the speed", "You shouldn't go for that job, stay with the one you have", "I don't think you should move abroad, it will be too expensive".

Changing destructive thinking patterns

The principal phase of changing is to acknowledge the issue. You will discover many individuals who simply don't think there is an issue or find it hard to admit their faults, so they see no compelling reason to change. For those people, then you are free to do nothing, but understand that you will always get what you have always got. Let's not continue to sail on the shallow waters of the comfort zone, because as we all know, this is not where growth happens. You have nothing to lose and everything to gain.

Everyone's perspective of the world is unique and it is from your perspective that your thinking patterns arise and your thoughts create your behavior. When you start to see and appreciate life for all the wonderful things that make this world great, then you will focus on these things and it will leave you with an enriched and colorful life. If you think life is awful, you will discover and focus on all the harshness and destructiveness of its existence. Change your thoughts and you truly change the world you are living in. Yes, it's not all sugar and spice and puppy dog tails, but what I am saying is that you can choose to focus on those things and see the good in every situation. There is a lot wrong with the world, but it is your perspective that defines your reality. If changing the world to a better place is something you are passionate about, for example, then you can do that through changing your destructive thinking patterns and show others that there is still good to be found in the world.

Do you think if you focus on the negatives in life, you will be happy and fulfilled in your journey to change the world and that you will succeed? You are not responsible for the atrocities in the world or the way it is, but you can have a positive impact and you can make a difference by starting with yourself and inspiring the people around you. To do this, you have to have the right mindset and see the world in a way that inspires others, by replacing our negative thoughts to positive thoughts. Start small. Start with yourself. Gandhi would say, "Be the change you wish to see in the world". If you do this, then your light will shine and it will inspire others to let their light shine too. It only takes one candle to light a hundred more. So the key is to change these negative and destructive thinking patterns into creative, positive thinking patterns. Some people just want to watch the world burn... with candles of positivity.

The first stage to changing destructive thinking patterns is acknowledging you are using destructive thinking patterns by being honest and open with yourself. The second stage is to be consciously aware of *when* you are using those destructive thinking patterns and the third stage is to *change* them to positive ones through reprogramming. The "I will" and "I can" patterns. We have talked about what negativity is and where it stems from, which is fear. We talked about the degree to which it may have crept into your life and then we went on to look at the 8 types of negative thinking patterns. Now it's time to focus on stage three, changing and reprogramming those negative thinking patterns to positive thinking patterns. Before we start stage three, let's look at the power of positive thinking and what it can do for you.

The power of positivity

Can you hazard a guess and imagine what the most positive, successful and upbeat individuals think about throughout their day, or more importantly, how they think? The answer is simple and straightforward... happy individuals are problem solvers and appreciators. They find solutions and go after what they want with enthusiasm and optimism, but are grateful for where they are, where they have been and what they have. They do not dwell on things that are out of their control or things that are stressful, they find solutions for problems and work at them. They gain pleasure from knowing they are on a journey of betterment, but can also appreciate where they are on their journey at the present moment. They find joy in the little things in life, the small, everyday things. They appreciate the ability to have fresh water for their morning tea, they appreciate the legs they have to allow them to walk to work and they appreciate what they have as they know many others are not so fortunate.

They understand not to take things for granted just because they have always had it, for it is luck and chance that they are born into the situation that was given to them and it is only through their perception that they can appreciate what they have. Some people often complain about their hardships, their job, their house or how bad things are in life, but it is always a matter of perspective. I always like to imagine what it would of been like if I was born 100 or 200 years ago. People don't understand that even the poorest people of todays developed countries live a life of luxury compared to how it was only 100 years ago.

Back then, the working conditions were longer hours and longer weeks, only getting Sunday off if you were privileged enough. There was little to no benefits, not to mention the unsafe and unpleasant work environments of the factories. If you injured yourself, there wasn't much given in compensation and it could leave you struggling to make a living because no one else would hire you. Even the hot shower you have in the morning can be considered a luxury as it was virtually non-existent. Back then people only bathed in warm (if you were lucky) water once a week and it was in a bath and it was usually for the whole family, with the man of the house bathing first, then the woman, then the kids. I don't even think I have to mention women's rights 100 years ago.

Then we look at technology and the advancements we have today compared to back then, where the electric vacuum cleaner, invented 1901, and a pop up toaster, invented 1919, was the height of technology and only affordable to the rich. Actually, forget your hot showers, sliced bread can be considered a luxury. Otta Frederick Rohwedder from Iowa first invented sliced bread in 1912 but it did become commercially available until 1928 where the machine not only sliced it but wrapped it in wax paper to stop it from going stale.

Today, it is hard to remember what life was like without the Internet and for some younger ones it is all they have known. Think of the arduous task 100 years ago of searching through 10 to 20 books just to find the information you needed, whereas now, you can find that information by hitting a few buttons on this plastic, metal box in front of you.

So you see, everything is a matter of perspective. The world is forever improving and you should try to appreciate the things you have, because at one stage it did not exist or was considered a luxury only affordable by the extremely wealthy. Take nothing for granted and see everything as a privilege, that's my view on life.

So that is an example of how to appreciate your environment and appreciate what you have in life through your perspective. Now let's take a look at problem solving and how to deal with negative events and negative energy that may be directed at you when you are on your positive journey. There are a couple of well-known individuals today who dealt with negative events from the get-go of their life and it will show you how they dealt with these negative fears and turned them positive to illustrate how problem solvers do not give up on their problems, but find a way to succeed.

Michael Jordan was not always destined to be an NBA player, let alone an NBA superstar. Growing up, Michael was the 'goofy' kid who liked basketball. He wasn't very tall and didn't come from an athletic family. What he had that kept him going was determination. Michael had many setbacks and failures throughout his career, but the hard work and self-belief eventually paid off. This is why we get one of his famous quotes "I've failed over and over and over again in my life and that is why I succeed". When Michael first entered the sport, his jump shot was not good enough. So he spent his off season practicing hundreds of jump shots every day until they were perfect. In High School, Michael was even rejected from the basketball team! For every weakness, Michael found a way to turn it into a strength and he never gave up. Today we know him as the greatest basketball player of all time. Do you think he got this way from letting negativity and fear of failure rule his life? Do you think he said to himself that he will never be as good as some of the other players in the league so he didn't put everything he had into getting better? Do you think failure of getting into his High school basketball team deterred him from his goals and dreams? Of course not, he turned his weaknesses into strength, he turned negativity into positivity, into drive and ambition.

Albert Einstein is another famous example of overcoming his circumstances and not letting those around him put him down. He did not speak until he was four, he did not read until he was seven. His teachers and parents thought he could be mentally handicapped, slow or anti-social. He was expelled from school and refused admittance into Zurich Polytechnic School. Think of all the negative influences he must of faced growing up, the lack of belief in him, especially from those closest. It was his self-belief and his ability to stick at problems in the face of negativity that earned him the Nobel Prize in Physics in 1921 for his discovery of the Law of the Photoelectric Effect, a law that is still used today to help make solar panels work. He also established the General Theory of Relativity in the same year he came up with the Photoelectric Effect.

The ability to solve problems and the power of appreciation are two of the most vital qualities a man or woman can have to be positive and improve their life. Sometimes problem solving takes time, effort and hard work but it will allow you to be successful, happy and filled with a sense of achievement. It is good to appreciate the small achievements as it drives us forward, like the small steps along the way to your goals. When you think about your goals and figure out a way that you can achieve them, no matter how long it takes, you feel more confident and more in control of your life, it gives you purpose and vision. "If you want to live a happy life, tie it to a goal, not to people or things" – Albert Einstein. The appreciation for what you have and what you achieved will make you happy, making your brain release endorphins, which gives you a sense of wellbeing. The combination of these two approaches, problem solving and appreciation, is a powerful combination indeed and as a result, they add up to a positive mentality.

Happiness in the journey itself

As we just talked about, it is important to set goals and achieve what you want in life through problem solving. I just want to highlight something so as to avoid any confusion. For most people, they look to the next goal or milestone in life *before* they think they can be happy. If only they had that or *when* they achieve that goal, *then* things will be better. Or *when* they move into that new house and *when* they get married, *then* everything will be okay and they will be happy and content. It is important to be happy in the journey itself, not only in small timeframe from when you achieved the goal. This what I mean by appreciating what you have achieved so far. You need to make sure you are happy during the process. You have to appreciate and gain happiness from the things you already have and from the journey towards your goals. Happiness is to be found in exploring, learning and experiencing as well as achieving. Happiness is not an elusive quality, it is readily available to anyone regardless of circumstances.

Let's do an experiment to show you how readily available it is and how you can call upon it at any time.

Okay, close your eyes for a moment and drift back to a special memory of when you felt happiness or joy. Smile and focus on that moment, let yourself experience it again and embrace that feeling. Get caught up in the memory and hold it for as long as you can. Did you do it? You might only have been able to hold onto that moment for a split second, but the point is, that happiness is available to you any time and you can use this to access it in order to change your state/mood. The trick is to practice changing state into the mentality of a positive person and recreate the mindset you have in that happy memory, so you can use this to be happy in the present moment and enjoy the journey. Changing your state, will shift your mindset and change your physiology to allow you to accept new experiences in a more positive light. It will take practice, especially if your negative mindset is strong and you have let it seep into your personality. You have to work on it, but it will be worth it and you deserve to enjoy a happy journey. Sometimes when I am not in a good mood or I am feeling stressed, I say to myself, "Life is good" and embrace that feeling. I think about something that made me happy and focus on it to change my state into a happier one. From this, I carry that feeling on to whatever I am doing at that time. This helps me to change to state and get back into a positive, optimistic and appreciative mindset.

Positive people are humble people

Positive people keep their mind on what they need, they find solutions to their problems and continue searching for approaches to get it. They are clear about their objectives and they are sure that they will finish them, even if it takes time. But they do not let these achievements turn into vanity or pride. They are grateful for where they came from, what they have in the moment and what they have achieved along the way and through this gratefulness, a sense of humility and empathy accompanies them. Positive people will have a love and self-belief in themselves that will allow them to share that love with others. They will be kinder, more caring and empathic towards others as they understand the struggles of life and understand that everyone on the planet has their own struggles they are dealing with. It may seem selfish that people focus on their own internal happiness first, but this is a necessity because you need to be able to love yourself before you can truly love others. This applies to relationships also, you have to put your own happiness first so that the love you have for yourself will shine through to your partner. Remember, if someone is happy, it does not mean that have not been through struggles themselves. They may have learnt to deal with their issues and they know how hard it can be, that is why they are so willing to help others in their journeys too. So do not be bitter or jealous towards happy and positive people, as you do not know what they have been through to get to that state. If anything, learn from them or ask them why they are always so happy. You might notice the humility in their answer and gain some knowledge which you can apply to your own life. Remember to learn from the experiences of others, as well as from your own and always remain humble and grateful for the experiences you have had, as others may not have had the opportunity to do what you have done or had the opportunity to have learnt from the experiences that you have had. This leads on to the next positive trait.

The power of positive thinking in learning

Confident, happy and positive individuals look for the significant lesson in each misfortune or mishap. As opposed to getting agitated or rebuking another person for what has happened or looking for someone or something to blame, they take control over their feelings by saying, "What can I learn from this experience?" Resolve today to build up that state of mind, learn from your experiences and when something bad happens, discover the lesson to be learned. It may be small, it may be huge, but there is always something to learn from people or situations. Even negative or foolish people, or someone you perceive as having no value, there is always a lesson to learn from others, so do not be quick to judge (remain humble). "I have never met a man so ignorant that I couldn't learn something from him" – Galileo Galilei.

Optimism is a positive person's trait

Resolve to see your glass of life as half full instead of half empty. I used to be a pessimist myself, I used to always see the potentially bad things in situations which lead me to be quite fearful of them. I was always very shy around new people and had a tendency to become withdrawn and quiet. It was only through my own journey did I learn how to become optimistic, to see and focus on the yin and not just the yang. I became happier and more adventurous. I don't see everything through rose colored glasses, I can see the good and bad in situations, I just learnt to focus on the good and the positive, which helps me to climb higher and bring more happiness and laughter to my life. I use the bad for good now, I understand the darkness in situations and I can use this to my advantage by turning it into something positive.

Staying positive through failure

I am the captain of my ship and everything I do is a choice and those same choices are given to you. You have power and control over your life and your situations. I firmly believe every human being on the planet is strong and powerful, some have just forgotten this fact because they have let life beat them down by judging themselves through the eyes of those who don't appreciate their value. But at any given time, the choice is still there, so choose to be happy. Choose to have some faith that a situation will turn out well and if it doesn't, well hey, you tried and you learnt from it, so it's never bad.

If you never fail at things in life, it means you never try new things. Have high expectations with respect to achieving things and don't be afraid to fail. People see failure as a bad thing, but it's actually not. It means you are putting yourself out there and we all learn from failure so how can that be a bad thing. Just as you choose to be happy, choose to not be afraid of failure. Understand that bad things will happen, things won't go to plan, you will fail at things, but this is a good thing. Use failure as an opportunity for growth.

Positive attitude development

It is easy to have a positive state of mind and to be merry when everything is working out as expected, but it is at the point where you experience unexpected misfortunes and troubles that you are tested as to how much you have developed the positive mindset. It takes a certain character to remain strong and positive in times of hardship, but this type of character is developed over time. Do not scorn yourself for falling back into negative patterns if you have been programmed that way through your journey, it will take time to rewire and reprogram your brain. You may find you are more up and down at the start, but that's okay. Slow progress is still progress. Notice and acknowledging these negative patterns when they reappear and rectifying them is the important thing.

It is an ongoing process and sometimes it takes time to develop positive thinking into a habit. Habit will become character, so the more positive thinking you do, the more it will become part of who you are and the less you will slip back into negative patterns. Never give up, always go back to the basics when you need to, learn to spot the thinking patterns and practice affirmations to believe in yourself and remember you are strong and powerful and you are in control of your ship and where you want to sail. If you find yourself back in shallow waters or getting stuck in the sand, start changing that fuel again to the type that will drive and push you back into open waters. Love yourself enough to want the best for yourself. Your negative thinking does not define you, it is your actions that define you, so even by the willingness to keep trying you are showing strength of character. Always seek to develop your positive attitude and nurture it so it grows. This positive attitude development will improve your character and make you a more powerful and strong person.

How to access the power of positive thinking

Our mind controls our actions. You can tap into the power of positive thinking by taking simple and straightforward steps to reprogram your mind. Every individual is equipped with a brain that is capable of reprogramming. By learning to change your thinking patterns, you can change the way you think and therefore the way you act. With a positive mindset, you can expect more happiness, bliss, joy, self-esteem, better wellbeing and success in your life which will likewise be accompanied with decreasing anxiety, sadness, stress and unhappiness. Fundamentally, whatever your mind focuses and thinks about, will determine the actions you take. Envision positive results and you will get positive results. Assuming responsibility for your mind and how you think is an important first step in the process of change. You can learn to change your mindset through repetition of confirmations, affirmations, goal setting, reflection and a form of meditation.

The force of positive thinking assists us with effortlessly seeing the open doors surrounding us and gives us the boldness to make a move when opportunity presents itself. There is a no more noteworthy state than a sound, positive mind. You feel invigorated, determined, optimistic, cheerful and in control. A feeling of prosperity pervades your mind. The future looks hopeful. It feels great to be alive. Embracing positive thinking as a lifestyle will bring useful changes into your life and make you more content, brighter, optimistic and more effective at going after what you want.

10 things you can do to start positive thinking

1. Smile and Laugh - It has been shown that smiling and laughing changes your state of mind, even if you force yourself to smile and laugh. Change your body language and you change your physiology.
2. Help others - Focus on helping other wherever you can. The best way to make yourself feel better is by making others feel better.
3. Clear your conscience - The human conscience is a perilous thing, it makes individuals condemn and judge others, so clear your conscience and never put others down, even in your mind.
4. Appreciation - Being thankful leads to humility and empathy. It also allows you to achieve happiness in the present moment.
5. Set goals - Set your goals daily on paper and make a short term and long term plan. Having small and big goals will give you the drive and inspiration to be successful at what you want.

6. Train your mind to concentrate on positive thoughts - Replace 1 negative thought with 3 positive ones and back up those positive thoughts up by taking action on them where possible.
7. Surround yourself with those lift you up – Spend your time with individuals who will inspire and bring out the best in you. Those who encourage you to go after what you want, even if that means following different paths in life.
8. Be committed – Be committed to becoming more positive and incorporate positivity into becoming part of who you are. See it out until the end, no matter how long it takes. Slow progress is still progress.
9. Work Out and Eat Right – Taking pride in yourself and your health is an important part of loving yourself. Go for a walk, run or some type of exercise. Find a sport or active hobby you enjoy. Take up dancing, rock climbing or yoga. Do something you enjoy.
10. Meditate. Practice meditation to relieve stress, relax the mind and focus on your goals

Advantages of positive thinking and being happy

- Lower anxiety levels
- Improved immune system
- Makes you mentally stronger
- Gives you the tools for success
- Brings joy through helping others
- Helps with your life compass
- Gives you influence over people and surroundings
- Reduces feelings of sorrow, discontent or sadness

Reprograming negative thinking patterns

We have covered what negativity is, how to acknowledge negativity, learning how to spot it, then we went on to talk about the power of positivity and the advantages that positivity can bring. What I am now going to focus on is reprogramming the brain to replace the negative thoughts with positive ones. This reprogramming will involve simple psychological techniques that will rewire your thought patterns through repetition. This can be done over time and will require effort and commitment on your behalf, but it will be fun and exciting to see how far you can take this and to see the results it will produce for you. Be optimistic and commit yourself. It starts with self-belief that you *can* do it and a conscious decision to decide you *will* do it and you *will* succeed. Reprogramming is something simple to condition your brain and you will be doing it in the morning, through the day and in the evening. The more you do it, the more it will become a part of who you are.

The technique is based on Hebbian theory and "Synaptic Plasticity", which is a term coined in neuroscience to describe the ability of synapses to strengthen or weaken over time, in response to increases or decreases in their activity. For those that aren't very science savvy, what this basically means is that the more you do something the stronger it will become. It mainly applies to learning and memory. So the more you practice the methods for positive thinking the stronger those thoughts and memories will become and thus, the more your brain will be primed to receive and create positive thoughts and the more of a positive person you will become. See, that wasn't as complicated as it sounded. It doesn't really matter how it works, to be honest, all that matters is that it works and it is proven to work. I hope I've impressed you with my genius, let's carry on.

Step one involves going into a passive state so that you can make decisions more calmly and objectively. Some people can have very reactive and emotional based thinking patterns, so this will be especially beneficial to them. Others can get very stressed in everyday situations or environments so this is a way to detach themselves from that environment so they can think clearly and objectively.

The second step involves reminding and reinforcing yourself of your commitment to the positive mindset and performing affirmations and positive thinking while you are in a relaxed and consciously aware state. We need to constantly exercise this processes so that we can keep our mind focused and spot the negative thoughts in order to reprogram them to ones of positivity and optimism.

Do you recall the sales example I gave earlier. Where you did not meet your sales bonus and you wanted to cry into your coffee cup. Let's see that example in a different way, by turning the negative into positive using reprogramming. When you acknowledge yourself focusing on the negative, such as complaining about why the sales went badly, worrying and stressing what will happen next or even just ignoring the situation, the key is to find the positive in the situation. To do that, you will use step one to relax your mind, like a form of meditation or mindfulness. When you are in state, you can now use step two so that you can reprogram that your mind to focus on the positive in that situation.

For example, you could see this drop in sales as an opportunity to better yourself. A chance to re-evaluate your skills and how you can improve them. An opportunity to grow, to learn. Be grateful for your job and the salary as others may not even have a job. Be humble enough to accept that maybe you are lacking certain skills and use this to take that course that the company offers, or an online course in marketing techniques. What will solve the problem, sitting there and pointing figures or being optimistic and taking action to the best of your ability to prevent the problem happening again? You will strive to better yourself and see the opportunities and potential for growth in every situation. This is one example of how the steps can help you to start seeing situations in a different and more positive light, by focusing on the positive. Let's look at the "Two Step Method" in more detail.

Step One

Tense and release.

Begin with this unwinding activity: Take a deep breath in through the nose, breathing in as much air as you can, then hold it. Now tense up all the muscles in your body, from your calves, legs, abs, back, shoulders, arms. Now breathe out slowly through the mouth and as you do so, slowly relax every muscle in your body in line with your slow exhale, feeling your muscles soften as you breathe out. Feel the stress leave your body with your breath, feel the stress release through your pores and body as you relax. Now again breathe deeply in through the nose like you did before, only this time you don't need to tense your muscles, instead you have to smile. Keep the muscles nice and relaxed and smile on the inhale. On the exhale, feel the stress leave your body through your mouth, your body and your pores. Feel it leave your body and drift off into the air, never to return as it gets swept away.

Repeat this breathing (without the tensing, just the smile) for as many times as you need, focusing on relaxing every muscle in your body and releasing the stress. Drop your shoulders, loosen up your body and focus on the air and oxygen inhaling into your lungs and circulating round your body, then leaving through your mouth, carrying out all the toxins and stress. This is just a simple meditation technique that is practiced in many other disciplines, but I have often found it is the simple, basic things that have the most impact. A lot of people use meditation for many different things and that is because it works.

Many studies have shown that if you compose your body to mimic the emotion you want, then your physiology changes to match that emotion.

For example, the power pose is a famous one. If you throw your hands straight up in the air, smile or laugh, like you have just won a famous victory, then your body chemistry and composition will start to mirror these feelings. It is the same with feelings of happiness and relaxation, imitate the state of relaxation through body composition and smiling and your body chemistry starts to mirror that state. This is why it is important to smile during this technique, so you can help change your state. It's a good tip for interviews, which everyone probably knows already, if you act and put on a persona of confidence, not only will the interviewers perceive you as confident, but you will also start to feel more confident too. Win win! The same principle applies to this meditation in step one, we do this to change our state to one of passive relaxation, so we can control our emotions and our state of mind.

Visualize your happy place.

I know this always sounds silly when you say it and it still sounds silly to me whenever I think of it, but that's a good thing because it makes me smile and it works, so I use it. While performing the breathing exercises and you concentrating on your breathing and the stress leaving your body, visualize being in your happy place. This may be on the beach listening to the wave's crash on the shore with a warm sun beating down on you and a cool breeze drifting over your body. It could be you walking through a forest listening to the sounds of the animals and the running water from the stream beside you. It could be you sitting with a loved one drinking a beer or wine. Whatever or wherever it is, feel it, see it and smell it with as much detail as possible. It is your happy place so be creative and imaginative, make it whatever you want as long is its somewhere relaxing, comfortable and stress free. A "Hakuna Matta" place, if you will.

The more you practice being in this place, the more vivid you can make it. You can practice going there even when you are not stressed, not in a negative state or do not even need to focus on anything. It is just to help you relax and be in a passive state. It's a form of meditation which can be used for a variety of different reasons. In this place you can be completely yourself and it allows you to feel secure, calm, passive and at peace. From here, you can make unemotional, objective decisions or it will help you wind down and detach from reality and give you a sense of stillness. It is also a technique used by many that have problems falling asleep, so if you suffer from that, this is a good procedure to get you to fluffy cloud land.

For those that think the beach or forest technique is too cliché, you can try a different approach, one that I use when I meditate. Close your eyes, see yourself entering a lift on the fifth floor. There is a keyhole below the keypad and only you have the key. You put the key in and turn it. You feel yourself gradually floating down five levels. Every level you go down in your mind, you gradually move away from the outside world, making you more casual, relaxed and calm than the previous level. The key you turned takes you to the basement level below the ground floor. Only you know of this place and you are the only one who can get there. On this level, there is everything can dream of. It is your place and you create it the way you want it. There could be a heated swimming pool, Jacuzzi and hey, this your room, why not have and full troop of kittens and puppies come flooding towards you as you step out of the lift. It is whatever you want it to be. It's your place to unwind, relax and destress. You are only limited by your imagination.

Spend however long you like here, embracing that feeling of peace and relaxation. When you are ready, get back into the lift and return gradually to level one. Let yourself know you will be conscious, alert, and refreshed when you arrive. You *are* strong and powerful and you *know* that you can conquer your fears and solve your problems (say it to yourself out loud if you need to). After coming to level one open your eyes and own your being. Carry yourself with pride and go out and take on the world with a smile. Enjoy the journey.

Work on going to this happy place at least twice a day, preferably once in the morning and once at night. Spend a minute, two minutes, or anything up to thirty minutes. The more you do it, the easier it will become and the more you will be able to call upon this place when you need it. This will give you control over your mind and emotions. I used to think all this stuff was too new age and hippyish. I consider myself a very rational and logical person and found stuff like this silly and embarrassing at the start. I still do sometimes, to be honest, but I roll with it anyway because it works. Its imagination and that is something we need in our lives. I'm sure you have all come across or heard of this type of technique before, it comes up in many areas, but I urge you to try it and practice it yourself if you have not done so before. Some of you may have experience with this type of thing in yoga or mindfulness exercises and if so, then use your own form of meditation to calm your mind before moving on to step two. Meditation and mind relaxation is something simple but as I mentioned it is usually the simple, basic things that are the most powerful and effective and have the most impact. It can take less than a minutes and it the first step in changing your state from negative to positive. How will you know if this will work for you? Well you have to try it of course. Nothing to lose and everything to gain. Your ship, your adventure.

Once you are in your happy place, it is time to transform your negative thoughts to positive ones. If you have a problem in life, or someone is making your life harder than it should be or you have a big decision to make, then this is where you can make the best decisions. It is the quiet place of the mind that allows you to hear that inner voice just that little bit easier. Trust that inner voice, because it will keep you right and it knows what is best.

From here, you can make the right decisions, not based on fear or emotion, but from objectivity, optimism and unlimited potential. So how do you know if your decisions are the right one? "You will know when you are calm, at peace. Passive." – Yoda. And yes, if you haven't figured it out, I am a geek at heart and I had to throw in a Yoda quote. When in our happy place, let's ask ourselves, what do you need changed in your life? What are your passions? What do you enjoy most? Is there something in your life that you fear and want to overcome? Should you go for that new job? Should you ask out that girl? Whatever it is, go to your happy place and find out. Your inner voice is waiting to answer you.

Step Two

Reprogram your subconscious mind

When you are in your happy place, that calm and relaxed state, you can begin your positive reinforcement and affirmations. It is a technique to keep you centered and focused on your goal or to detach from the hectic hustle and bustle of the busy work environment or the stressful situational or social environment that is engulfing you. In time, you will not need to go to this happy place to make your decisions, you will achieve this state naturally and learn to make decisions and opinions without the meditation. But to get us into habits of the right mindset to have, then this is what we will use as a tool until then.

Those who are successful, will naturally be passive, objective and relaxed in their decisions. For example, do you think Mark Zuckerberg, founder of Facebook, when he hears the latest security or potential hacking threat, loses his mind and starts running around grabbing his employees shaking them violently screaming, *"What are we going to do?! What are we going to do?! We are doomed!! Run for your lives!!"*

I am going to take a wild guess here and say no. Instead, he will remain calm, assess the situation and start coming up with solutions, like gathering the lead teams on the topic and devising a plan of action. You must have the mentality of a leader, to remain in a relaxed state and think of solutions and come up with a plan to overcome obstacles. You must know that you *will* handle the situation and you *will* defeat your problems, this will take the stress out of problem solving as you know it's only a matter of time.

Rules for Reprogramming Your Subconscious Mind

When in the happy place, you will follow the simple rules of thinking positive. Never state anything to yourself as "I won't/can't _____". Continuously state things in a positive manner such as "I can/will/am_____" or change the whole statement around into a positive one. Example: "I will be afraid to do that bungee jump and will end up having to come back down", will be expressed as, "I *am* brave and I know I *will* do that bungee jump and I *will* feel amazing doing it. It *will* be an amazing experience."

When choosing what you need to do and after you have your positive assertion in your mind, say it out loud. If you cannot say it aloud (if you are in a public place), then repeat it over in your head or better still, write it down. Use a piece of paper or Word/Notepad document. You don't have to keep it, you can delete it or throw it away after, though I recommend keeping it, but writing it down and repeating it is important. If you are doing this at home and you write in down, keep that bit of paper on which you wrote it. Carry it around with you as a constant reminder of your goals.

Be a person of action. Get a pen and bit of paper now if you can and start by doing this experiment. Write on it, "I *have* a positive mindset and I *will not* let negativity rule my life" and "I *will* continue to write down my daily goals". Now carry this around with you in your pocket, your purse or wallet. When you start to notice yourself being negative or you want to focus on your goals, take it out and look at it. Say it to yourself out loud, then return it to where you kept it. What you focus on, you attract. If you focus on becoming more positive, then it will be so. Having things written down is a concrete reminder of what you want to achieve.

During your reprogramming sessions, express your positive assertion boldly like you know it to be valid. Use the body language I talked about to change your physiology to mirror the state of that which you want to achieve. Relax, shoulders back, head up, chest out (not too much), feet shoulder width apart (pointing out slightly), smile. If you want to go one further, do the power pose while reciting your affirmations. Convince yourself! Believe it and believe in yourself! It couldn't be anymore simple, move and feel like you are in a position where you have already achieved your goal and imagine being in that position and enjoy and embrace it. Visualize it. Act and behave in a way that's congruent with the person you want to be. Believe in it and you can achieve it.

Planning, goal setting and finding solutions to your problems are an important part of positive thinking, but don't forget to make time for that other thing I told you about earlier in the book, which is also important. Can you remember what it is? If you have, good on you, you have been listening. If not, that's okay, I'm here to remind you so that you can focus on it. That other thing of importance is gratitude and appreciation. Gratitude and appreciation for the things you already have and for the small things in life. Write down on paper 3 things that you are grateful for and carry it around with you. Let's look at some examples of reprogramming using this "Two Step Method".

Examples of Reprogramming

Example 1: You have a fear of dogs and when you think about them you get tense, stressed and fearful. Use steps one and two to breathe and release the tension and stress. Relax yourself and go that happy place and while you are there, see yourself petting and playing happily with a dog. Feel your face grinning and make a smile appear on your face. You feel glad. You see the canine wagging his tail and he is glad to see you. You feel the soft fur under your hand. You notice the scent of the dog. Say to yourself "I *am* happy around the dog" and "I *will* enjoy the love and affection that the dog gives me in return".

Example 2: Imagine you are about to do a bungee jump. Visualize yourself there in a positive light, you are on that stand about to jump, you are excited to be there, you feel amazing that you are about to achieve something you never thought possible. You stand in your confident pose, chest out a little, relaxed shoulders, and head up. You jump and shout with exhilaration and excitement. You imagine and picture yourself sitting in your friend's house after it all, having a drink in the buzzing atmosphere with your friends, "I'm so glad I done that. It was an amazing experience!"

A good time to practice the Two Step Method

In the morning time when you wake up and at night time before you go to bed are great times to meditate and say your positive affirmations and concentrate on reprogramming as these are times when you are most relaxed. They are good times for writing down your affirmations and goals for that day or the next. You can review and reflect on how well you did that day and you can plan on the positive day ahead. Slow progress is still progress, so focus on the positive, even if was only one or two things you done well. Forget about the negative that happened, it is irrelevant, what you want to focus on is the positive and how to increase these. What you focus on you attract, so don't focus on the negative. The brain and willpower is a wonderful tool and just like your muscles, the more you use them, the stronger they become. So the morning and night are good times to practice the Two Step Method, especially to start you off, but you can also practice and use this throughout the day as well. The more you do it, the more your mind will start to focus on the positive and it will become part of who you are.

A final thought for reprogramming

In the wake of practicing this reprogramming two, three or however many times a day, your subconscious will start to be wired to react in a more positive state towards people, situations and environments. The more you do it, the more your brain will be rewired to the conditions you set for it. You should start to notice results after the first week and you will start to notice you do not have to reinforce your mind so much with conscious awareness and meditation. Your subconscious will start to take over in time through practicing and it will become part of who you are. The less you will have to meditate and the more it will become natural. You will no longer be that negative person and instead you will evolve into that positive, happier achiever who goes after what he wants and finds solutions to his problems while maintaining a sense of humility and appreciation for the small things in life and for what you have and where you are.

The power of self-belief and becoming the best version of yourself

I have mentioned self-belief while talking about positivity, but I have eluded to the fact of why it is so important or how to gain self-belief. Everything you do stems from self-belief. It is the catalyst for action, without it, or by limiting it, you are holding yourself back from becoming the strongest version of yourself and becoming powerful. Self-belief helps you become capable of inspiring and helping others around you by demonstrating that no matter how hard life gets you can survive the storms and conquer the seas, enjoying the journey along the way. I will now discuss how self-belief works to assist you getting what you want by having faith in yourself that you will achieve your goals. This section will help you with moving from wanting to have confidence in yourself to really trusting in yourself and utilizing the astonishing force of self-belief. We will begin by investigating the systems of self-belief and their advantages.

Why is Self-Belief important?

Here are some of the main benefits that self-belief provides:

1. Opens the doors of opportunity
2. Gives you focus
3. Makes you active, committed and motivated
4. Inspires others to believe in themselves too

Opens the doors of opportunity

Self-belief assists you with seeing the open doors. Why would you try and go through a door if you thought it was locked? What about if you thought it was an empty room, would you bother going into it? Having a limited belief in yourself limits your possibilities, it shuts off the world around. Having a strong belief in yourself and what you can achieve allows you to imagine a world of possibilities that your mind would otherwise have dismissed with a convenient excuse. Doors that you previously would have considered dead-ends will now be open to you. With more doors open, you can now set about walking through those doors and taking action, turning possibility into reality. I firmly believe that I can do anything if I put my mind to it. Nothing is out of my reach with hard work and dedication. To me, if a door is locked, I'll kick it through. Metaphorically speaking of course, don't be going round kicking doors in, you might get into trouble.

Gives you focus

Without self-belief in yourself, you will approach a goal or objective with disbelief, you will feel nervousness, hesitant and unsure. You will become stressful and worry on the failings and therefore you are more likely to never start, to give up or to lose interest. Your ability to succeed is directly related to your ability to believe. With self-belief you will be sure that you can do it. You will have a drive and determination just not possible without it. Once you believe you can achieve your goal, it will lead to a sharp focus on that goal and you will devise a strategy and follow through with the implementation of the steps to fulfill that strategy.

I'm sure you have come across the saying, "What you focus on, you attract". Buddha puts it this way, "The mind is everything. What you think, you become". For me, I relate by thinking of a real-world example. When I went for my motorcycle lessons, one of the first things they teach you is to look in the direction you want to travel. So if you want to U-turn, you look back up the road in the direction you want to ride. If you get nervous when turning and stare or look at the curb, that's where the bike is going to go and you run the risk of hitting or crashing into the curb. That's why they tell you in your lessons not to stare at the curb. It is the same with your focus in life. If you focus on your goals, your direction and where you want to go, you will follow that path and it will lead to success. Alternatively, if you focus on the negative and all the bad things that can go wrong then it will go wrong and you will crash into the curb and attract the failure that you are trying to avoid.

There are two types of failure you should be aware of when reaching for your goals. Temporary failure and permanent failure. What do I mean by this? Well on your journey to success, you will fail many times, but with focus and determination you will keep picking yourself up and go after your goal again. Until you give up, failure is only temporary. Remember the Michael Jordan quote, "I've failed over and over and over again in my life and that is why I succeed". Those that have self-belief will learn from their failure and chalk it down to experience, it will not sway them from their belief that they can achieve what they want. Every successful person knows you have to fail many times before you succeed. Do you think successful people have a positive perspective on their failures, or a negative one? Failure is just experience gained. Keep your eyes on the prize.

I stumbled across a video before of Perry Cross and it has stuck with me to this day. The video looked like it was taken by one of the guests at the dinner party, but I am very glad that they decided to take out their phone and record it, because it had a big impact on my life. He talks about your focus in life. Perry cross suffered a horrible rugby accident when he was 19 which left him as a quadriplegic. He talks in the video about when he was on life support after the accident and when he was lying in the hospital bed. He couldn't move, couldn't feel anything, couldn't breathe, he was paralyzed from the neck down. Perry couldn't even eat, drink or talk. All he could do was see and hear, the communication between doctors, family and friends was extremely limited. One can only imagine what was going through his mind at those difficult times. In the video, he talks with raw emotion about the time he lay in the hospital bed soon after the accident, when his mother approached him by his bedside, knowing the hardships and limitations that of what this condition would entail for her son, leading to a life of potential suffering. She asked him with all the gentleness and love that a mother has, does he want to go on. He had to make decide whether it was worth it.

"My mum come to me and said, 'would you like me to turn the life support off?' I had to make the decision to say no and fight on. But it's got to be worth it, it was up to me to say I want to fight on. But there had to be something to live for, there had to be a reason, I couldn't just take up everyone's time".

Perry went on to live life to the fullest, to inspire others and found the Perry Cross Spinal Research Foundation. He was also friends with Christopher Reeves. His story is a truly inspiring one, one that I encourage everyone to look up, he is truly a positive and inspiring individual. The reason I bring him up, apart from his influence on my own life, is to highlight his self-belief and how this led to him having to have an acute focus on his goals. He explains in the video about focus, through the analogy of a magnifying glass. He says,

"Every success I've had in life is by persistent focus on the goals I have set. Imagine a magnifying glass in the sun. If you wave it around, nothing happens, it doesn't do much. You take the same magnifying glass and focus it on an object and what happens? It starts to burn, it has power. I believe our mind is the same as that. You focus that magnifying glass and it has power. Focus your mind and its got power".

Makes you active, committed and motivated

Now that the doors are open and you have that razor sharp focus, you can take the consistent action needed to follow through with your goals. It's difficult to make a move towards a goal if you don't genuinely trust you can accomplish it. Your goals could require hard work and effort and with self-believe you will have the determination and perseverance to succeed. It all starts with belief. You have to believe before you can achieve. Sometimes you just have to trust in yourself that you will succeed. The future is unknown, but with self-belief you can see yourself as successful before it has actually happened. See yourself as successful and it will become so. It may take some time, but carry yourself like you are already there and you will manifest the results into your life through the hard work, focus and persistence. Self-belief and commitment is a requirement of success.

Inspires others to believe in themselves too

Self-belief is infectious. By being strong and courageous in who you are, you will inspire others to do the same. It is not easy to be yourself, it can create a lot of resistance from others who do not share your views, even hostility and friction. Sometimes it can be mean losing people who are already in your life. But this is okay, you are always in control of your life and the direction it takes, so don't be afraid to lose people as you will gain new people in your life that share your values and goals. Through attracting the right people into your life, you will be able to support each other and progress in life. You can be anyone you want to be, but it takes hard work and sacrifices. In the end, it will be worth it. You will have created a life that you wanted, which will allow you to be happy, positive and appreciative. Only then can you inspire others through the shining of your inner contentment and happiness.

Sometimes people or family can hold you back in life. I am not one to subscribe to the traditional family values in that just because someone is more closely blood related that this somehow honors them privileged rights. I have always seen the bigger picture and been of the understanding that we as humans are all one family and that respect should always be earned. I take people at face value and judge them on their character and not on their relatedness to me.

Respect should always be earned and there are those close to you that are destructive to themselves, others and you. This is not to say you should not try and help them, if it's within your power, but that help could arise from inspiring them by being your happy, self-loving and successful self. You should help all those who cross your path, this way. Do it through inspiration and being the best person you can, never compromise your integrity. Never let people lead you astray or do things that you do not agree with. Self-belief requires you to love yourself and want the best for yourself, even if that means separating yourself from people who are holding you back. You are not responsible for other people's lives and you cannot change someone who does not first want to change themselves. You should lead by example, have the strength to be proud of who you are, especially in the face of adversary. This all comes from having self-belief. By doing so, you will inspire others to better themselves. I think all people are strong and powerful, those that are destructive or negative are not living their potential and this is why they are bitter and resentful. It is not your job to fix these people, but if you do want to help others, you need to invest time in yourself first and become proud of the person inside of you.

Creating Self-Belief and Confidence

There are 5 approaches to help you gain and build your self-belief and confidence. We have discussed the power and functionality of self-belief so now I can show you how to create and build this confidence in yourself. Before I tell you the secrets of gaining self-belief, I have another little secret I'd like to share with you first. Would you like to know what it is? That secret is…. I've already taught you the secrets to self-belief *gasp*. That's right, I Miyagi'd you. Let me explain. Self-belief and the positive mindset are one. They are mutually inclusive. Like 2 sides of the same coin, you cannot have one without the other. I covered the main principles of learning self-belief by how to eliminate negativity in the mind and how to create a positive mindset. The mindset of a person who loves and respects themselves. Let's go over these principles to recap what they were:

1. Self-belief and a positive mindset are learnable

The wonderful thing about both happiness, positivity and self-belief is that it's achievable by everyone, it's only a matter of choice. You can learn the positive way to look at yourself and the world by becoming aware of your thinking patterns and by being able to recognize and acknowledge the negative thinking patterns and converting them into positive ones. You can decide if you want to look at the world in a positive or negative way, it is always only a choice. Your self-belief and positivity will make you stronger, happier and more successful. Life can be a bombardment of negative energy but it is your perception of yourself and your inner dialogue which determines your perception of the situations, people and environment and ultimately how you view the external world. You must realize that we are all strong, powerful human beings, every one of us, with the capacity and potential for helping others and shaping the world around us, it is only when we are not realizing that potential that our capacity for self-belief diminishes. People can fall into a negative spiral by losing their self-belief and not being the best version of themselves. Don't let the negative influences of the world around you chip away at you until your self-belief turns to self-loathing. Learn how to deal with these situations and learn how to see the world around you in a positive light, by learning first, how you see yourself.

2. Seek to improve yourself and realize your potential

Always seek to improve yourself. Focus on the things you want to improve on by writing down your goals. This can be done many ways, like having long term goals of what you want to accomplish and smaller goals that will help you reach those long term goals. Daily goals are very important and a great way to help you focus on what you want to achieve, such as writing them down on a piece of paper and carrying it around with you as a constant reminder. The task I gave you earlier in the book, was to write down "I *have* a positive mindset and I *will not* let negativity rule my life". So remember when writing your goals to use the correct language, such as *I have, I will or I am*. By wanting to improve yourself and realize your potential you are demonstrating your love for yourself in wanting to become better. You are showing self-belief and positivity.

3. Visualize a powerful version of yourself and develop your character

You become the person you want to be by carrying yourself in that manner, both physically and mentally. Prime your mind to visualize who you want to become and make it part of who you are by acting on those traits and qualities. The example I gave, was imagine yourself going for a bungee jump. To visualize yourself there in a positive manner, standing on the edge about to jump, you are excited to be there, you feel amazing that you are about to achieve something you never thought possible. Then later that day, to picture yourself sitting in your friend's house after it all, having a drink in the buzzing atmosphere with your friends, "I'm so glad I done that. It was an amazing experience!" I'm not saying do a bungee jump unless that is something you really want to do. I am using that as an example of vision and potential. Be your own motivator, set yourself some challenging tasks and believe that you can do them. Think positively towards that goal and becoming that person. Life can be fun if you make it. "The way to gain a good reputation is to endeavor to be what you desire to appear." Challenge yourself and you will become stronger and develop character traits that will improve your quality of life and help you achieve success. Qualities such as Humility, Courage, Confidence, Gratefulness, Tolerance, Selflessness, Honesty and Persistence to name but a few. By thinking positively through knowing you can achieve and develop yourself, you are showing self-belief and self-love.

4. Set goals and continue your upward spiral

People that have a positive mindset and believe in themselves will go after what they want by settings goals so they can achieve and climb the ladder of success. Many people are caught in a downward spiral of failure. They let the world get the better of them and they slowly lose their passion and joy for life, resulting in them losing self-esteem. Small failures and negative thinking has allowed them to be conditioned into accepting these failures and they have lost the belief in themselves that things should be better. Though positive thinking patterns and goal setting, you can reverse that downward spiral into an upward spiral. Succeeding at the small goals will set you on a cycle of success, each one exponentially adding to the last, reinforcing this new identity of a successful you. Like a snowman's head rolling down the hill, your momentum will gather and grow. Your willpower, like the muscles in your body, will grow the more you work it and the stronger you will become. Your self-belief and self-esteem will rise as you achieve your goals.

5.   Problem solving and appreciation

The way to build your self-belief and to be positive is to be grateful and appreciate what you already have and what you have already done. To find joy in the little things in life, the small, everyday things, then you filled with a sense of humility, allowing you to develop empathy and connection with others. As mentioned earlier in this book, you should appreciate the ability to have fresh water for your morning tea, and appreciate the legs you have to allow you to walk to work. Understand that for whatever you have, there are others out there who have not. For everything you take for granted, there is someone out there wishing, dreaming, suffering or working hard for it.

The power of appreciation and the ability to think objectively and critically to solve your problems can aid in creating and building your self-belief. When you are appreciating something, it makes you happy, your brain releases endorphins, which give you a generalized feeling of wellbeing and this encourages your mind to have self-belief and happiness. You add to a positive mentality. If you do not appreciate what you already have, you are not going to appreciate what you get. Gratitude is a quality of someone who has self-belief and a positive mindset.

Find your passion in life

Finding something you love doing has an amazing impact on your whole life. It's like a raindrop landing in water, it creates a ripple over the whole surface, spreading out endlessly. Finding your passion will spread out into all areas of your life, giving you drive and motivation. The hardest part unfortunately, is discovering what you love. For some of you, you may already know what that is, all you have to do is listen to your inner voice and go after it. For others, it may be slightly harder and a matter of trying new things and doing some inner searching. There are ways you can help discover your passion by trying new things and looking back at different times your life. Here are the ways I helped discover my passions in life and why it is important to follow them. Hopefully they will help you too on your own journey.

1. Rediscovering your gifts

What are you good at or have a natural aptitude for? Disregard what you may good at but you don't generally like doing it or get pleasure from, because that is not a passion. We want love and passion as the verb to describe it. I'm talking about the things you have a talent or gift for where great enjoyment and joy occupies you and feeds your creative child. By that, I mean you have genuine fun doing. "Working hard for something we don't care about is called stress; working hard for something we love is called passion" – Simon Sinek.

Are there things you get pleasure from doing that you don't believe you are good at but other individuals have complimented you on? Maybe you ignored or rejected their compliments. For example, do you love taking pictures or photos? I'm not talking selfies sticks here, I'm talking about seeing the hidden beauty in the environment around you. Taking photos of city lights at night with a moonlit background or small blooming flowers that emerged from a cracked sidewalk? That type of thing. Maybe you just want to grab your camera and capture that expression on a face, so you can relive it. If this sounds like you, then maybe you have a creative talent for photography you need to explore. This is the type of inner passions you should explore and consider.

I believe we are all creative beings, from cooking to art to photography to problem solver, we all have a creative element about us. Creativeness can come in different forms, such as organizing social events and gatherings. If you can find where that creativeness is, then you are on the right track to finding your passion. Let's take another example. Maybe you are always the one that loves to gather your friends together? To join people up and enjoy the social interaction at events or gatherings. Then maybe you have a creative passion for organizing.

When I was solo travelling last year, I met a man in a hostel in Vegas. When he spoke about his job, he talked with so much excitement and passion. He was an events party organizer for high end clubs and parties all around Las Vegas. He said he had the time of his life. Yes, he said it was hard work and tough at times, but he also said it was worth it and wouldn't change any of it. He took pride, a sense of achievement and satisfaction in being able to throw these lavish parties and connect people. He said he met people from all walks of life. To me, that was his passion. You could tell by the way he spoke about it.

You don't necessarily have to start off by being great at what you love doing, that will come through time as you develop your talent and skills. You just have to have the courage to follow your passion and explore your potential. And you know what, if you try something and it doesn't work out, who cares. At least you tried, you went for what you wanted and you gave it a shot. That's something to be admired and respected. I guarantee you will never regret being courageous and trying new things in your search of your passions. In life, you regret the things you didn't do, rather than the things you failed at.

2. Be Proud of who you are

Have the confidence and respect for yourself to be proud of who you are. Everyone is different and everyone has different strengths and weaknesses. Your negative thinking about yourself may stem from your own insecurities. Learn to acknowledge these insecurities, only then can you face them head on and take action to work on your weaknesses and improve yourself. I am a firm believer in self-improvement and self-development. Your passion or going after that passion may be blocked by the fear of embarrassment of fear of being judged by others, so learn to be proud of yourself and follow whatever those passions may be, even in the face of those fears. When you value yourself, you want to improve and when you work on improving yourself, then you get a certain sense of pride and achievement. It can be hard to be proud of yourself if you know there are areas you can improve but you do nothing about them, so make sure to take action.

I love bodybuilding, it's a passion of mine, but if you are going to worry about what people think of you or compare yourself to others then you are never going to get anywhere. You might not even make it to the gym because you are worried of others judging you. I have heard people tell me before that they wouldn't go to the gym because they are too unfit. This baffles me. You go to the gym to get fit but it is their fears of people judging them that holds them back. They think people are going to look down on them or laugh at them for not looking their best when they are sweating on the treadmill. You should do it for yourself and be proud of working out for yourself and no one else.

I am one of those people who suffer from poor genetics in my calf muscles. I have high calf insertions which means the area of my calf muscle is limited to where the calf muscle actually starts on my lower leg. This is genetics and no amount of gym training can change your insertions. What I can do however, is focus on and improve the muscle that is there, by making it grow, which requires a lot of work. Do you think my fears of people judging me stopped me from my passion for bodybuilding? Hell, no. I'll never have the best calves in the world, but I'm still proud of them because I worked hard on them to grow them bigger.

Never compare yourself to anybody except yourself. There may be others out there that are better at something than you, or more fit, or have a better physique, but all you can do is work to become better than the person you were yesterday and never let your fears hold you back in life, especially when it comes to things your passionate about. Nobody can measure effort but yourself, so always seek to develop yourself. People may mock you or judge you, but as long as you know you have improved and put in the effort to improve, then that is what ultimately counts. A wise man once said, "Haters goina' hate". Let them do their thing and you do yours. "Nobody can make you feel inferior with your consent" – Eleanor Roosevelt. So be proud of who you are and what you want in life. Value yourself and do what makes you happy. Try new things and you may find your passion lies on the other side of fear.

3. Think of what you liked to do as a child

This is presumably the most straightforward approach to uncover where your passion may lie. Before the adult in us tries took control, most of us knew precisely who we were and what made us happy. What did you enjoy doing most as a child, what are your happiest memories? Maybe this is in an indication of what path you should take. Could you say you loved horses and horse riding when you went on those family trips? Did you love painting or drawing? Maybe you could sign up for a painting or horse riding lessons. Did you love singing as loud as possible until individuals begged you to stop? Maybe a career in music could be an option. You don't have to become famous to consider yourself successful at your passions, there are many singers or musicians you may not be well know, but they love what they do and they bring happiness to others through their music, which gives them more enjoyment and fulfilment than anything money can buy. This to me, makes them a success.

Make sure passion and inspiration are your drivers. Look back to your childhood to find what really made you happy and go after that with the intention of bringing your gift to others. Think to yourself, "What gift can you give to the world? What talent do I have that can make others happy?" Referring back to Jim Carey's famous speech:

"I wished people could realize all their dreams and wealth and fame, so that they could see that's not where you are going to find your sense of completion. I can tell you from experience, the effect you have on others is the most valuable currency there is. We are not the avatars we create. We are not the pictures on the film stock. We are the light that shines through, all else is just smoke and mirrors, distracting but not truly compelling."

4. How do you spend your free time?

Unless you live on another planet (which for a few people I know could be a distinct possibility) then you only have 24 hours in your day. On average, according to the American Time Use Survey, 9 of those hours are spent on your job related activities, 8 of those hours are spent sleeping and 2 hours are spent on cooking, eating and doing housework. Now considering you are not in your dream job yet, then that is 19 hours taken up, leaving us with 5 hours of time to spend on ourselves and to spend doing what we enjoy.

What do you do with your free time that you enjoy? I don't mean watching TV or playing the computer. You could enjoy these things, but mainly they are time-fillers, something to distract you from the real world or from boredom. I am talking about the things you love doing in your free time that you wish you had more time to pursue. Maybe it is something you do on your days off when you have more free time or maybe something you look forward to doing when you are on your holidays. Start to focus and think on these types of activities and make more time for yourself to follow these passions. Invest time in yourself. Is there a way you can use these passions to earn money. Can you make a career out of it? Try and fill your life with the things you love doing. It terms of a career, it is better to earn less money doing something you love, than making money and not being happy. Don't get stuck in the trap of money over enjoyment.

For me, my current goals and passions are bodybuilding and gaining financial freedom through my passion for helping others. This is the reason I decided to write this book, to share my knowledge I have gained over the years on positivity and the correct mindset to live a happier, more rewarding and successful life. In order to do this, I had to invest time in myself. I had to use those limited hours of my free time to research, write down a structure and plan, I had to figure out how to create an eBook and hardcopy, how to create a book of high value that will help others, how to market the books and how to publish them. I started acting on my passion to help others while exploring new ideas and ventures.

Success for me has not always been a driver, I had lived a life of passiveness, unsure of what I wanted to do or where I wanted to go. It has only been through my journey for self-improvement that I *learned* to believe in myself and that I can achieve whatever I put my mind to if I work hard for it. This gave me the drive to start asking myself what do I want in life. I have always liked helping others and building people up. I was always there for my friends when they were down, to help change their perspective and see their problems or issues in a more positive light. I would use the experiences of others as well as my own, to become stronger and wiser. So it was through my journey I explored different areas and tried new things to see where my passions lay.

I consider myself a thoughtful, caring and knowledgeable person. People have often said jokingly, you should write a book on motivation to help others. So that is exactly what I did. I realized that I had a passion for helping others and this was one of my gifts which I could give to others. This book is my attempt to extend that help and motivation to others. Part of the time I invested in myself for self-improvement was spent reading books, watching videos and practicing what I learnt. Hopefully if this book adds value to people's lives then it will be popular and more people will buy it. Thus, it will also help me in gaining financial freedom by doing what I love, helping others.

For you however, you may have your own unique goals, objectives and passions. Maybe you always wanted to set up a business, maybe your goal is finding the right person. What time have you invested in yourself in exploring your potential passions and achieving your goals in line with these passions? What effort have you put in? Are you fearful of exploring your passions or are you going after it with love for yourself because you deserve to be happy and to achieve? Have you researched and explored your goals and passions, whether that is to start your own business, for example, or finding the right person or how to improve yourself? Whatever drives you and gives you a sense of joy, then go after that.

There is a wealth of information through books and the Internet, all you have to do is focus your mind and it has power. Explore new things and if you think something might be where your passion lies, then focus on that, even it will require some hard work. Think positively about exploring new areas in your life and invest time in yourself by taking action on it. If you don't know how to follow your passion, then find out. In the Age of Information, ignorance is a choice. So have no excuses and invest time in yourself and don't let anything stop you from finding your passion because once you find it, it will echo into all areas of your life and give you a sense of fulfilment. Remember that you have to be happy first before you can make others happy. Time is a rare commodity, love yourself enough to do what is right for you. Go after your dreams and passions. They are waiting for you.

5. Don't let fear hold you back from your passion

As we get older, we can easily get caught up in the "daily grind" as it's called. It is times like those that we need to remember our inner child and remember to have fun and remember that life should be a playground to be enjoyed. This is why it's so important to to follow our passions so we can enjoy life. Don't take life too serious. Yes, we all have responsibilities and commitments, but we need to remember to have some fun as well. Don't get caught up living in the past or the future, dwelling on things that cannot be changed or worrying about things that have not happened, enjoy the present. This is how you are going to discover your passions and not be afraid to follow them. Fear as we have learnt, holds us back in life and stops us doing the things that truly matter to us. But fear is only a thought. Unless there is actual danger, fear is only a construct of the mind that serves no purpose except to hold you back. 95% of the fear you experience is imagined, so you have the choice whether to give in to fear or not. See it as a challenge to face and overcome and smile while you do it. You can live your life through fear, which can stop you enjoying your journey, or you can live your life through love and unlimited possibilities. "Everything you want is on the other side of fear" – Jack Canfield. So don't let fear hold you back in exploring your passions, use it as a tool to see challenges and overcome them, which will make you stronger and develop your character as well as help you discover your passions. There is no bravery without fear, so enjoy the journey of overcoming fear in search of these passions and do it with a smile on your face because you are showing bravery and determination, this will make the journey more fun and enjoyable.

One of my biggest fears in life was competing in Kickboxing for the first time. I had practiced Kickboxing for about 2 years and loved it. My technique was perfect. But I thought to myself, what does having the best technique in the world mean if you have never challenged yourself in a practical way through competing in the ring and facing an opponent who could have equally as good technique. Will I still have that perfect technique in the face of a real life opponent, will I stay composed or will I crumble under the pressure? It scared me to the very bone to compete and when I did sign up for a fight, I would sometimes lose sleep over it at nights. It seems a contradiction to love something that you fear, but because I feared it, I wanted to face it and conquer it, I wanted to challenge myself and get out of my comfort zone. I had a goal that was hard and that is where the most sense of achievement and accomplishment is to be found. It was this process of improving myself and taking my passion to the next level and conquering my fears that I enjoyed and which improved my confidence and self-belief.

So I was determined to get into the ring and I done exactly that, I faced my fears and I fought in my first Kickboxing show... and lost. But I tell you something, I walked out of that ring with the biggest smile on my face that no one or nothing could wipe off. The winning or losing did not matter to me, what mattered was that I conquered my fear and I did. It was the best thing I had ever done in my life. It turned out, I was so nervous leading up to the fight that my legs were like jelly. Kicking was one of my strengths, but I lost points for not kicking enough, which I think swayed the decision in his favor and so I lost on points. It was a battle for the full 3 rounds, we went to war and I wasn't giving up, I fought as hard as I could and that is all that mattered to me, I gave it everything, I gave it my best shot.

My friends from the Kickboxing club were all very proud of me as well and all of the people I spoke to said I should have won, but to me I did win for stepping in there. They also said, "Why didn't you use your kicks?" I have a video of the fight and you could hear my friend in the background with her powerful voice shouting, "Use your kicks! Use your kicks!" It always makes me laugh. Yes, the kickboxing fight was hard and leading up to it was even harder, but you learn to deal with the fears and not let it rule you. What you fear you attract, what you face disappears. I went on to have another 8 kickboxing fights and 2 MMA fights and I won them all.

It was a fun time, I learnt a lot about myself when competing, but most importantly, I learnt to face my fears and see it as a challenge. I learnt to turn the negative energy into positive energy by seeing it as a way to improve and better myself and I learnt to have fun while doing it. I look back on it with such pride and it has made my journey so much more rewarding. The sense of friendship and comradery at the kickboxing club was amazing. We all supported each other and helped each other. That was in between the sparring sessions when you beat lumps out of each other of course, but that was fun too. Before and after the bell, you were back to being best friends. And I wouldn't have it any other way. So by learning to change my mindset to one of positivity and self-belief and by facing and conquering my fears I learnt to follow my passions and it bring excitement and happiness to my life. So whether it is stepping in to the ring to compete or starting up a new business, don't let fear hold you back from following your dreams and your passions in life.

Positive thinking positive life

I hope this book has helped you understand the mindset to see the world from a positive perspective, a perspective of someone who loves and believes in themselves and someone who does not let negativity rule or control their life. You now have the tools to take action and gain momentum in changing your mindset by eliminating any negative thinking patterns and replacing them with ones that will enhance your life and give you the fuel to reach new levels of success and happiness. I once heard that there are three sorts of individuals in life: those that ignore it, those that watch it and those that get it done. Make beyond any doubt you are the person who gets things done. Take control and steer your ship in the right direction. You are the captain. You are in control. You have the power to make the decisions and to decide what journey you will have.

I have told you why you are drawn to negativity and why it seems so appealing and why it is easier to go along with negative patterns. Don't let the bombardment of negativity from the world creep into your being like damp in an old house. The first step in changing is to acknowledge the negativity and negative thinking patterns. Only then can do anything about them. You can spot these negative thinking patterns and reprogram them into positive ones by using the Two Step approach of calming the mind and focusing on replacing those thoughts into positive ones using the right mindset and through your internal dialogue, language and belief system.

Positivity and self-belief is an unstoppable force once you harness the positive mindset. It will allow you to become more confident and skilled at facing and solving your problems. You will create and build that positivity and self-belief through changing your thinking patterns which will in turn allow you to become more powerful and successful while also remaining humble and grateful for the journey you are on. It all starts from how you think about yourself and the internal dialogue that you have. If you change how you perceive yourself, through your positive mindset, you will change how you perceive the outside world. Love and respect yourself enough to want to change and be more positive through your choices. You can achieve your goals and dreams and be more grateful, humble and appreciative of what you have. With self-belief and positivity there is a world of possibilities out there, so have fun reaching for them. Don't let fear hold you back and be positive in all areas of life so you can become the strongest version of yourself and live a life of passion.

Everything in life is a choice so if there is something you are not happy with, you know that you can change it through hard work and effort. Practice through the means of repetition, making the right choices by choosing the positive mindset over the negative one. Use those subtle differences in your inner thoughts that I told you about and write down your goals and reminders and carry them with you to help you focus. It will require some hard work and effort, but if you focus your mind you can make positive thoughts a habit. Nothing in life worth having comes easy, so if you want to change something about yourself, then you must put in the work. Once you reach and achieve that positive mindset I guarantee it will stay with you forever and it will become easier to think and behave with positivity because it becomes part of who you are and you will see how much it will enhance your life for the better.

More and more people are *learning* to switch to positive thinking in the understanding that it will not only reshape their identity into the powerful and unstoppable being that they are meant to be, but it will give them the happiness and inner peace that they deserve. Learn to move to a place of love. Do not let fear rule your life anymore. If you feel stuck, you will ask yourself, "What is it that I fear?" You will see the situation as an opportunity for courage and an opportunity to better yourself and to achieve your potential. Never put people down, but instead seek to inspire and motivate one another as this will help bring joy into your life.

We are all sailing in the same waters and have the ability to help those that are stranded by passing on this knowledge and by living your life as an example of what life can be like with the right mindset. We can choose at any time to eliminate our bad habits of negative thinking and reprogram ourselves to be more positive and see the world through different eyes, or more accurately, a different mind. Our eyes are really only the viewers of information, it is the mind and our conscious decisions that interpret that information into our own story. Who will write your script, fear or love? What story will you have?

I hope you now understand the power of positive thinking and how it will help you get the most out of life. It helps you to be excited, enthusiastic and focus your mind on the important things that matter to you in your life in order to create the life that you want. You will be able to manage and solve your issues in the present and look back at things that happen along the way as positive experiences. By sharing the positive mindset and what you have learnt you can help others to better themselves also and you can equip them with the tools to have a more fulfilling journey. That is my goal with this book, to help others and improve lives, even if it is only a small improvement, then I would consider this book a success.

So make sure you create your world by *how* you think and from this *take action* to achieve your goals, shaping yourself into the person you want to be. "It is not who I am underneath, but what I do that defines me" – Batman. You and you alone are responsible for your life, so don't fall into the cycle of blaming the world around you when it serves no purpose for you. It is your decisions and actions that will determine your improvement and the quality of your life and who you become along the way.

A Stanford Research Institute study concluded that achievement is 88 percent positive thinking, and just 12 percent education. Positive thinking is a critical element in your capacity to succeed in life. Positive thinking is a hopeful perspective that gives you the courage to take action towards reaching your goals. It is a mental state of mind that will create results and bring you a sense of fulfillment, joy, peace and wellbeing through the process of improving and bettering yourself. It allows to make strong connections with others and brings accomplishment into your life.

While we all have this capacity for change, it is ultimately a choice. I will now leave that choice up to you. You will know if this mindset will change your life by practicing it for yourself. So do it with passion and optimism. Get out there and take on the world. Life is too short to spend it sitting on the couch watching the days drift by. Life can be so much more than that, like a child seeing the world for the first time. Apply the knowledge you have learnt because if you do not apply it then it is as good as useless, like knowing how to read but never haven read a book. When you apply this knowledge, I guarantee that you will have control over life and you will be able to handle and achieve the things you want. The world will not seem like such a threatening place, instead it will become your personal playground full of potential. The choice now lies with you.

"If there is no enemy within, the enemy outside can do us no harm"

Thanks for reading "Positive Thinking Positive Mind:
The Mindset"
I hope to see you again soon

If you enjoyed this book or found it useful, please show your support by leaving a review

Phil Hunter Publishing 2015

ISBN-13: 978-1519509086

ISBN-10: 1519509081

Phil Hunter Publishing

137 Oval Road

London, NW1 7EA

22289457R00043

Printed in Great Britain
by Amazon